T0152090

MAKE   YOURSELF   HAPPY

ALSO BY ELENI SIKELIANOS

(Published by Coffee House Press, unless otherwise noted)

Body Clock

The Book of Jon (City Lights)

The Book of Tendons (The Post-Apollo Press)

The California Poem

Earliest Words

The Loving Detail of the Living & the Dead

The Monster Lives of Boys and Girls (Green Integer, National Poetry Series)

to speak while dreaming (Selva Editions)

You Animal Machine

CHAPBOOKS INCLUDE

The Lover's Numbers (Seeing Eye Books)

Poetics of the X (Rodent Press)

MAKE YOURSELF HAPPY

Eleni Sikelianos

COFFEE HOUSE PRESS

Minneapolis

2017

Coffee House Press books are available to the trade through our primary distributor, Consortium Book Sales & Distribution, cbsd.com or (800) 283-3572. For personal orders, catalogs, or other information, write to info@coffeehousepress.org.

Coffee House Press is a nonprofit literary publishing house. Support from private foundations, corporate giving programs, government programs, and generous individuals helps make the publication of our books possible. We gratefully acknowledge their support in detail in the back of this book.

Library of Congress Cataloging-in-Publication Data
Names: Sikelianos, Eleni, author.
Title: Make yourself happy / Eleni Sikelianos.
Description: Minneapolis : Coffee House Press, 2017.
Identifiers: LCCN 2016027518 | ISBN 9781566894593 (softcover)
Subjects: | BISAC: POETRY / American / General.
Classification: LCC PS3569.I4128 A6 2017 | DDC 811/.54--dc23
LC record available at https://lccn.loc.gov/2016027518

PRINTED IN THE UNITED STATES OF AMERICA
23 22 21 20 19 18 17 16   1 2 3 4 5 6 7 8

for us: our past, present, and future

CONTENTS

HOW TO ASSEMBLE THE ANIMAL GLOBE

William Carlos Williams said:

              "Come on!
                       Do you want to live
forever?—
         That
              is the essence
of poetry.

  . . .

         For the most part
                it consists
in listening
          to the nightingale
            or fools."

MAKE   YOURSELF   HAPPY

THROUGH THE LOWER window I see
a man pass his bald
head is ecstatic in that way
it can be smashed
in a second shining bound
with drunk flowers & hot
to sing himself human O
human head stuffed
with ideas and
noises good and
not good   which I say
(good)   which I say
(not good) the syntactical violence inside a head
Beast head   Get on a donkey
and learn some grammar Get on a donkey
and ride

MAKE YOURSELF HAPPY

You walk into the sunlight
to make yourself happy.

This is the poem that will tell you
how to live.
It's set in Paris, so
you'll eat a croissant
to make yourself happy.

Here, we utter hexameters rarely.

We do confuse what is a command and what
a prayer
statement and threat, question
and answer.

Animals utter indivisible sounds so
often yet
Aristotle does not call any of *them*
a letter. Still, an
animal sound will
make yourself happy. Listen to this
kitten. We can call its noises an alphabet without confusion.

And here, you cannot be maimed by the muses.

See leaves in the gutters and salted butter that stands in a bright
rectangle of light like a small giraffe never melting in the sun which
is what you picture when your aim is
to make yourself happy.

You eat a lot of things to
make yourself happy. Stick this
piece of meat in your mouth to
make yourself happy. It's a good one. The sounds of

sirens outside the window are
gay to the ear that tends
to hear what it needs
to make itself happy. An interesting thought
about dirt or air or water will work
to make yourself happy. Look
from where you are (inside the window) not
where you want to be (outside the window), i.e., to
make yourself happy. This is the way we've come

along the dusky boulevards
like eager huskies, taking big steps, eating up
the sidewalks with our big-stepping big-licking legs
making ourselves happy. Tomorrow
we'll learn all the things to undo in the Making Ourselves
Happy school. First,
the hero/ine never moves towards death.

WHY WAS I SMOTHERING small raccoons. Comical now, but not so under the spidery gauze of sky. We were the bodies moving below misunderstanding like lumps of saddened [damaged, weakened, wounded, lacerated, suffering, insufferable] coal. My ribs turn in their sockets, axle sideways and burst to tell it: the huge raccoon on hind legs thumping on the top of the car. What is this animal encounter, what, this animal misunderstanding. All raccoons are enemies. (They survive as well as we do.) ("The use of weapons for protection…from aggressive animals is a…morally neutral action" [Survivalcache.com].) It looked so evil when I killed it, but once it was dead I saw it was no bigger than my hand. What is this animal anger. That is the question. What, love? What if it were The Last Animal on Earth?

WHO did the blue school
who bruised the wound
who had the goddess of love in her lap
to make herself happy—make
a village of love for your shadow
to live in so that
your shadow and your shadow's friends may be
unlonely living with all other *ombres*
I'm giving away all my belongings
in language   to make myself happy   must start
with "my language"   then find
chains of correspondence
for the world's every articulate hand and finger
(it's what touches the world)
a shadow *hombre* shows me the way toward the deepest umbers
like having an orgasm in your
happy

I HAD TAKEN THE LONG WAY HOME, the really long way.

I traveled to the edge of the human continent. There, I couldn't tell the difference between the insurgents and the Mennonites. The Shaker girls wore blue-evening-light dresses and danced in a circle speaking of the widow they had neglected. We went to the website of all acts of poetry, a huge screen at the very edge of the room, a bit basement, that seemed to grow little by little (would it overwhelm the scene?) when you pointed out to the dawn on the rightside horizon and my eyelashes made a shadow I could see. Will the screen engulf the world?
will the web?

was the widow their window?
what is an act of poetry?
Catching the light
with the side
of my eye.

the horse says neigh
the human says y(e)ay
a grasshopper, you said
will never be sad.
That's the first thing.

I BOUGHT SOMETHING, it was
A fancy thing. The man called me madame and
Opened the door with a swish. I was sure I had never been
So happy to buy something, my
Feet felt happy even though
The thing was for my wrists.

I HAD TAKEN THE LONG WAY home through all the wrong towns. Through dusty streets to get my daughter, got lost trying to take the short way home. Along the way I overhear someone asking for me on the other side of a door from the other end of a phone. That's me, I say, taking the receiver from a man with a muddyblond ponytail. It's the last office on earth, shipping and receiving tiny mutations in the survival-vowel sounds. Ah, hoo. I do make it to school, where a Japanese lady buys me a tan-colored latex blow-up boob because mine "are really so uneven," a state I'd never even noticed. O tiny things, like Delaware, and hours, turn us toward new states of thinking/being/doing. Anacreon says:

> I won't touch Amalthea's horn (cornucopia).
> I don't want to live 150 years (like Tartessos' king).
> But totter through one tiny hour of wine-bred bliss, yes!

> Yet

> I would not wish to live anywhere, ever, where everybody's always happy.

SEVERAL SITES OF FAMILY HISTORY

It has come to me to write of heroin again.

How my brother fucked up his inside and outside worlds then stitched them back, slow.

≈

"I was haunted by that face," the lady said speaking from memory of my mother's—"it was so sad, so troubled, so ill." I had never seen that face, had only seen my mother's.

≈

I'm in California again, the one in which the rain never stops.

After the rain, the green.

≈

We are trying to decide between pursuit of property or of happiness, but can't tell which.

≈

Then it has come to me to speak of heroin again.

How my father or my sister fucked up her face.

She was seeking relief not happiness.

≈

THE BOOK IS THE HOUSE where the bodies are buried

the book is the catacombs where the corpses enumerate

the book is the joy is the place where the copses unfold happy, fragrant, & shining

the book is the meat sliding inside the bear and the bear inside its blanketing fur

the book is the joy was lost on the horizon

as hours flooded in

the trees kissed across the distances, & the sun

mirrored

in its pages the lake

therefore lung-ed as any animal I leaf

the wide pages flammable with life

WHAT I MEAN and what I meadow

What I want and what I winnow

When I see it it's Sappho biting into a sesame seed

She arrives right through the centuries

Walked from Mólivos to Pétra

Bright blossoms along the way

Green fields seaside and some rundown stone houses among the hotels

Sappho, how's it going

Everything's great, I recognize

The sun   but where have our gods gone   Never

Mind, so much hiding the meat, giving them the fat

Now I can piss in the garden

I can throw my book in the sea

Drink my wine

Without wondering which meadow will winnow me, what girl

Like a rosy apple will make me

Sweet-mouthed, happy

Here I am eating ordinary bread! Leaping out of that terrible habitat

(the past) I can pluck & pluck

Her maidenhead

From the top of the Present

Maidenhead tree

DO NOTHING FANCY

I shall do nothing fancy
to make myself happy. Help!
I dwell here because I do not dwell
among the dead. But sunlight
is lethal to some, so shall I
make a golden ring that replicates itself or build a golden
hour from which is banished grief to
make the hour so roundly happy? Some will bind
themselves in beautiful things and some
in chains. Some made a fetter from
>   *–the sound of a cat's footfall*
>   *–the beard of a woman*
>   *–roots of a mountain*
>   *–sinews of a bear*
>   *–breath of a fish*
>   *–spittle of a bird*
but what kind of beard?

Name your fetter   name it *Gleipnir*
(a manacle as smooth and soft as a silken ribbon)

>   call it the wolf-joint   or call it the wrist, it is
>   where the wolf or the world will bite.
>   (put your hand in its mouth as a pledge)

>   Now: *How will you settle an argument* with only one hand?

wrist   wreathe   wrest   writhe   wr — to twist
the human mouth makes the movement-sounds
twisting out of the bindings
twisting away from how
make yourself happy moving
freely towards the experimental sky
and language the false start to love is

A HAND is an endangered antelope sheering through the ruffled grasses.

Thus the saga of the finger commences and continues, a zigzag across the joints that gapes between the stitches. *Pas joli.* The body splits. Despite the sad finger, a little sun shines on the façade slung across the day, having broken through the city's rough gray top hat. What do I do here? Wander, hang laundry. Admire the glistening streets. It's nice of you to admire our avenues, the city almost says, or forgets to say. In a big museum I saw a centaur brandishing a quadruped. I saw *la période finale, froide et parfaite* of a famous painter, which took place in a painting of a woman making lace. Later, I learned about the Pencil of Nature. To make yourself happy I try to smash the light right into my brain.

WHY BECAUSE the lost cat ate tiropita from my hand
why because I can see the other side of Lesvos from here
why because I saw Sappho in the rocks by the harbor saying plash plash Aphrodite
how could anyone not gorge always goddess and gorgeous
Sappho was looking great, profiled out to the east
why because of course the miraculous bees
They are surviving here they are
Surviving here

IN THE CAFÉ OF LA GRANDE MOSQUÉE de Paris the sparrows balance on the chandelier and swoop down where two old women have left their crumbs; the waiter swishes his hands and they disperse but later two young ladies will feed them from their fingers and the birds will cluster like dusty brown lightbulbs of warmth on the brass. The window's amber glass gives a diamond cutout into the world which is one I wouldn't want to be in — leafless and gray with frozen *flaques* on which to slip and bust your ass, and everyone inside's a bit gray, too, as if the sky's cold hand had caressed then invaded the face. Still, it's my world and I go into it, which is strange to say since every moment before the great lazy suspension and every place is — here I am, already in it. Now a cook comes up, he looks Bengali and cracks a menu at the birds who scatter for a minute then return to sharpen their beaks on the chandelier's chains for which no gold was dug up from earth's dark mines. Crimes.

Fact, shine.

WHEN I CAME HOME there were buds on the lemon trees and big light fisting through
the window—nothing
happier

To make yourself happy make
no error
ever

make no razor
mark   let no
razor mark be made
upon you

JUAN, JUAN ET SU FILS? said the dream.
Have a drink in the ancient Roman light that flares
on the strange American faces
on the airport train. Juan, Juan, my
countrymen and women, no offense but
how did you get so
fat
gray
badly cut
unread
small-eyed
woolen
while I was away? I was gone and when I came back
you'd voted for the wrong politicians! So many men!
Had I slept for five minutes and found you
on the subway saying all the wrong things or
in the meadow to the starlings?
You'll feel like the waist of an otter in the teeth of a tiger and wonder
how hell is dressed with poorly—
how it's haunted by badly pissed-off persons or people
These people, for example, forgetting
to make themselves happy
built the entryway but forgot to build the building
used up all the wood & coal & sky & ice & light
Now *¿Dónde viviremos?*

TO MAKE MYSELF HAPPY IN THE FACE of error I repeat
bandicoot long-nosed bandicoot. You
try it. And see how happy
is the b, the oo. A little mud
on the windows doesn't matter when you've got
one in your mouth, she said, smashing
the cigar. Buh-oo.
I look out the window.
There are no bandicoots there.
I'd made such a trap of sounds
in the poem and scared them
away from here. Still, there is surely someone nearby
begging for beer money which is how
he makes himself happy. But when I am sad
I look through the pine trees and think
of children who are hungry
somewhere, this poem
can't feed them. That is not
a right way. Right away I think
of the man in a big house & his
wife, maybe they have children. It should
make them happy. To be
ravening before our bowls of food.

SEE the happy ring in the pond around my
                    daughter & my sister swimming there
   The pond around the ring around
               my daughter & my sister swimming
and the land around the pond around the ring
           around my daughter & my sister
                    swimming there

If you took a picture from here you could almost see the craters—
        landing sites from Apollos
           12, 14 & 17
                 along with the last foot trails left on the moon
(from the Lunar Reconnaissance Orbiter Camera you would see them better)

If you took a picture from the moon you could see
       the ring in the pond
       around my daughter & around my sister swimming

You could hear my daughter ask,
           how old are you
You would hear my sister say,
           23

You would hear a crackle in the pick-ups
Then you would hear my daughter tell
       I have 25 *dollars*

You might hear the ripple, you might hear the ring, the dust
blowing across the crater

THE HAND THERAPIST

In the hand world, all sens-
ation is sutured at the tips.

Flexor digitorum profundus
A chiasmus, a crossing, she says, we call it
Zone 2, No Man's Land, tap
taps the knuckle. I know
horses are making the crossing from the
superficial to the deep
tendons where they make the
X after the bone, thirsty.
She wants me to know but maybe
She doesn't want me to know too much.

      When I describe the world
      this is about the body.

Your finger is making layers and layers of scarring
like forty strata of stiff Saran Wrap, enough
for New Jersey. You're making
enough for ten bodies, I'm trying
to slow that drapery down and
smooth it so
things can slide around.

Anne told me Cecil Taylor once swaddled himself
in Saran Wrap and wandered the halls
of the Boulderado otherwise
naked. I believe
the manager asked him to leave or
at least return to his room.

The body can manage a sliver of glass
but there are other foreign entities
that flummox it, the Hand Therapist says and my hand
heats on the table like
Cecil Taylor's wrapped physique
under the ceiling lights.

She taps my finger's tip
This is the most sensate
part of your body. Open.

In the hand world
she says again
the tendons cross deep in the flesh
She is my Hand Therapist
with an accent she brought with her from Virginia
just as you would a pocket full of acorns.

Dreamt: split rail fences, healing scars,
railroad tracks.

The next time I see her the Hand
Therapist cries and
tells me to wear gloves
all the time. Then she says
your scar tissue feels
real good. Must feel like Cecil
Taylor in cellophane tapping
on 88 tuned drums but
my stitched finger drops
the stitch into
decay and can
no longer open the good jar of tomatoes.

What damage the hand can
wreak on the world the world
gives back to it.

TO MAKE HERSELF HAPPY she stopped
struggling with the rope
that was tied to the tree
whose branches ventured
into the neighbor's yard and
was caught on the fence. Sun-
light kicking the needles
on the pine hard. Some straight
human-made things (like fences)
put on the hurt, if
banged into. I think I'll go
make something with my bum
hand to curve it up. Curving it up
in a loaf of bread just like the wind
or a beaver is never straight. It
makes herself gay to say so.

ESSAY: HAPPY BRAIN

Every turn of limb or feature, in those whose motions have a visible impact on the general happiness,
will be noticed and marked down

—Charles Darwin

How Happy Are You? (Likert Scale test)

I feel that the future is overflowing with hope and promise

Less True ○────────○────────○────────○────────○ More True

See the center flower
of the brain happy See it
sliced happy happy
hippocampus happy anterior cingulate cortex
a labyrinth, the brain
unspools its stiffening threads like copper wires untightening from
the trouble spot   happy *nucleus accumbens* happy *insula*

I think the world is an excellent place

Less True ○────────○────────○────────○────────○ More True

Dura mater, hard
mother, peel back to reveal
what   without my fist in its mouth   makes
rappers and Csikszentmihalyi know: for happiness, Be in the *flow*.

```
┌─────────────────────────────────────────────────────────────┐
│  Life is overflowing with rewards                             │
│      Less True  ○────────○────────○────────○────────○  More True │
└─────────────────────────────────────────────────────────────┘
```

If the world could stabilize
the word could   or if
                        the word no longer feeling
the world   went mindblind

```
┌─────────────────────────────────────────────────────────────┐
│  All past events seem extremely happy                         │
│      Less True  ○────────○────────○────────○────────○  More True │
└─────────────────────────────────────────────────────────────┘
```

My father kept pushing the lever, the
pleasure-center lever, my brother
kept pushing the lever, my
friends   was it
desire or pleasure
wanting or liking? Now
he's dead, my
dad.

http://blogs.du.edu/today/news/seeking-happiness-could-make-individuals-
depressed-2

Some women brought the domestic
into the poem like you would bring a blade of wheat to a field of grass   It went
feral & changed it (the field) without
domesticating the field itself and

I have done everything I ever wanted

Less True ◯————◯————◯————◯————◯ More True

makes me crazy with happiness.

Take this happiness test. Are you kind

to monkeys, to rats? Let's slice some
to find out. The mind, said the Dalai Lama
is trouble.

What makes a cow happy makes me
hungry. In the cabin, I kill
the fly.

"Gross National Happiness
is more important than Gross
National Product."
By: HM Jigme Singye Wangchuk.

"I'm happy I read this book!!" (Amazon review: *The Science of Happiness*)

In the United Arab Emirates there is now a Ministry of Happiness
"You can be happy as long as you keep your mouth shut."

No

                chaos   refugees   workers war

O how a word can hover in its surroundings between sense and sorrow
                          a narrow sound shivering
    as if the world itself rushed in decay toward that trembling

the what self in face of the other exchanges toward
      pain (knowledge) &
      pleasure (knowledge)
"climbing from the love of one person to the love of two"
and also shamelessly the accessible sky
forthright, untied

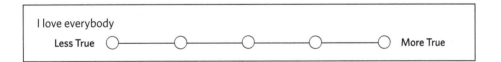

Earlier
I was feeling the hot sun on
my right hand while
driving it was

making myself happy—a pool of warmth in the webbing between thumb and index
like a Bermuda of pleasure that spread to the whole machine—but
worried
about liver spots—as if
that organ could rise
to the surface
of the body and kiss
the world hello so
happily   to see it
after too long in our
darks / out / our
depths

The whole world looks beautiful to me

Less True ◯————◯————◯————◯————◯ More True

SOME OF US got lucky

       Some of us got sick

     Some of us got mothers

       Some of us got rich

Some of us learned everything

    from the cities stretching below the skies

       where women & children & men desire

Proud Bird (diner, L A X)   whatever it is they desire

     & what have a right to

     what get

YEAH A MOON jelly would make a
good wedding dress—*dendraster*
eccentricities—
swallowing pebbles to make themselves
heavier   (so they don't wash away in the surf)   [sand dollar typo: *heavenier*]

brother Joe says:
cookies will make you happy
wrist the size of a cat's neck
everybody's there to make themselves happy
being silent   dharma punks could do it
the bouba-kiki effect until the end of time said other brother*
cops with beach towels bungeed to the backs of their bikes
Happy Donut is everywhere, said brother one (the one
        working out the opiates)
my friend's mother let out of jail eating strawberries by the side of 101 outside King
City—that's my property—that—that happiness

* Which shape is bouba and which is kiki?

"ONE WAY" into these woods
the sign says and
"no parking" as if
I'd want to park my carc-
ass in a patch of snow
a fuzz of white pine sapling says *yes yes*
in the wind then
no no!   when it says *yes*
and when it says *no* make a
go of
it. *It*
is how to live.

HOW HAPPY is the leaf, the
lamb   the deaf
ear at the mirror

IF THEY ASKED ME TO INVENT A DREAM

I am walking down a narrow street
I leap
into your arms
your arms are the poem
and I am the poet
how wonderful
to meet like this
right on the street, stranger!

IT'S A SATURDAY. We (me and Charlene) panhandled enough money to buy some Hostess Pies, a Heath Bar and a coke, 1976 or 5. We're just outside the Isla Vista market, laughing our heads off, about to get high on sugar. One of those men we've seen around town (yellowing brillo hair, not much taller than us) walks by, says (bitterly), "You're happy now, but just wait, wait till you're older." The laughter dumbs out of our fat-lined 11-year-old bodies for about 10 swift seconds, flopping on the sidewalk under the fog-blanket, weak sun, then *struts* back up like a baby monkey to its mother and we laugh harder than ever (the man disgusted), nearly falling on the ground from it. *Our happiness baffles what's trying to get in.*

TABLE 1. Sample blogposts in the U. S. happy/sad corpus, happiness studies [highest frequency words]

[happy]		[sad]	
yay	86.67	goodbye	18.81
shopping	79.56	hurt	17.39
awesome	79.71	tears	14.35
birthday	78.37	cried	11.39
lovely	77.39	upset	11.12
concert	74.85	sad	11.11
cool	73.72	cry	10.56
cute	73.20	died	10.07
lunch	73.02	lonely	9.50
books	73.02	crying	5.50

"You have noticed that the truth comes into this world with two faces. One is sad with suffering, and the other laughs; but it is the same face,"

I WISH YOU a tidy sum of pleasures
say, the syllables of a wolf and their continentally changing vowel
and stress; such treasures—

                           but how should we distribute them   across the days?

           as an army of   armadillos   tumbling
           in sunlight   ten thousand
happinesses pluraled up heaped and wait   upon you   *the surplus*
when the total of pain is subtracted   *from pleasure* (Bain)
the wery hunter to fynd his happy prey   OR   *Any happy concourse of Atoms*
He…Weenes yet at last to make a happie hande By bloudie warre (Gascoigne)

Test the "happiness factor" of any action
               How strong is the pleasure?
               How long will the pleasure last?
               How soon will it occur? (Bentham)
               How does it allow for lynching or beheading a man to make the crowd happy?

    In the felled light   find you
the happy set of liberty, plenty, and letters (Middleton)
bouncing in the noontime
swoon
when sun
won
all we ever wanted to win honey
suspended in the aspirated day honey   Have we achieved
       the greatest happiness of the greatest number (Hutcheson)
the exultant position of the

                                   new lover

on the hook of the h just as it leaves the body

      Ha

   Ha

         coughs it

       laughs it

               ha

ppy

        and so

you happy

    round as a berry

        or a bug

the color happy

      hanging on a branch

  in blue

        you

haul happy around

like a log   *Oh*

Happiness! Our being's end and aim! Good, Pleasure, Ease, Content! Whate'er

thy name! (Pope)   A trap

it was

The American Way. The prolific birds

gulp grain in the neighbor's nonspecific yard
& know nothing of it, though the neighbor
who puts seeds in the feeder is scientifically
American. To be
looking past leafless scraggly-ass
branches across a nonartistic low chain-
link fence prettied up with lattice & into
a strategic American yard? There is war there. And a cherry tree. May I claim
on our small (<1/4 acre) lot another hieroglyphic
territory? Make a different
happiness list? There is nothing
to be done about the anachronistic power lines,
the metal chimneys pointing out of roofs like turbine
erections, the 7 billion eudaemonistic humans. Take a lesson
from the squirrels. They never give
up being squirrels. About the drug blimps, the dust road smoothed
each night looking for immigrant footprints. About the war dead and the dark. *Have a
little dark or
have a little dog* (Palace) Have a little squirrel
or have a little twirl. If I can't occupy America
where can I   teach
specific felicific calculus
it has come to me to speak
happiness
come to me
when I speak of the world
terrific

    happiness that often madness hits

MAKING THE BIRD HAPPY

House finches bobbing on the branches
like fitful punctuation marks, comma in a puff of snow, blobs
of feathered exclamation
points bouncing
in the cold. They
decorate the view and entertain
the cat with red-winter tail feathers and caps. But
an hour later they're gone. How/where
did they go?

They're in the back of the bird book
with low "burry notes"
The red-shafted flicker who was also in the tree gives
a soft muffled *bwirr*
contact call, a clear *keew*
close contact call, a soft lilt
     wik-a-wik-a-wik-a

Every beautiful bird is in Texas.
Indigo bunting.
Lazuli bunting. Look at that bird's
bright-blue forehead!

Say's Phoebe says
     pidiweew, pidireep, pidiweew

a phoebe never mistakes herself
for a bird   she will never mistake herself for someone's happy nest

"that's not the way the bird would see it"   soaking
            in ultraviolet spectrum,   magnetic fields,   sunset's polarized glow
      a feather drab to us hovers in bird-world in pearlized light

yet when Parker plays "Ornithology" even the cat looks up
belief, the bird is happy
to the bird I keep applying what I think I know

CIVILIZATION would
make herself
happy if she could. She tries
some. A wheel, a
sanded piece of wood, pasture butter. I'm having
such a good time in civilization, she says, I better
text someone. To build a bolder, better Face
book, I try to hit it
with my voice.

Gustave Flaubert's father
had a voice like a scalpel, able
to skin the feeling right off
the surface of the body
with a word. He must be
just like civilization.

EVERYTHING in this dream is hard to read, because it's a dream of you. I flop down in the passenger's seat and email my secret boyfriend who seems to be something of an authority, a Black man with dreads and somewhere to be. Could he please bring me my walking shoes? With glue gun and wood I can make something with all the seams showing—a new road? Through the wasted charms of these deictic cities, find or found emotions as collective property

The you of *you* floats   an edge cut by   me
Please bring me

my good walking shoes.

AS IN A DREAM A WOMAN chasing another

woman cannot reach her, nor can the woman in flight

escape her pursuer, so I never

seem to arrive home   happy

could not overtake

nor could I pull it away, happy or grief

                                                  stuck to the heart or the face

When the great Master of Pursuit

Death and when

And when sleep came

brimful of happiness, in a soft bed

As in a dream a woman chasing another

cannot reach, so

the mind rushing over life

was trying to feel where the soul was—

base of the skull / top of the neck—no—

that's just a knot of tense muscle—a

twisted bone. I take

a twisted bone for home. Take it home. I polish it.

We are a truth for life's fracking. I guess. I caress.

Howl is   short for   how to say

                                  what's (long i) live

                                  what's glow

Blest beyond earth's howling bliss.

"MOST AMAZING   most amazing
happiness,"   says the teenage girl on the
cell phone on the bus, so

culturally saturated with meaning

later I eat a fancy meal
at a fancy restaurant   cooked
by a friend   then
in the morning   "millions
of poor Americans" can no longer
buy two gallons of milk a month, just one
(http://www.nytimes.com/2013/11/08/us/cut-in-food-stamps-forces-hard-choices-
on-poor.html, Nov. 7, 2013)   Reed says
two things arrive in the mind

          bump

how to live   smashing
like a human drone
into the sliding door   that's
the future   Try
swimming now
before you break the glass;

Make yourself happy
Insurgents & Men

in what joy-stores do you
buoy
so excelling in the yippee that you luminate the faces
of even oatmeal boxes   grenades   in shadows?
In ebullient jade-like nova light you levitate the pancakes
and all my sweet hurrays take flight
shed light
shed light
Shining honey, activate, make yourself of *jouissance*
in the common nominate noontime and the midnight

Do this with shadow
Do this with shade
Do it with sad light

It will turn you
from a money-lover
to a honey-lover.

Which
would you rather?

WAKE UP THE WAVES & CLOUDS IN CA

To be clouds or to beat clouds
You can decide
Which would you rather
There is a middle-aged woman doing somersaults in her van parked by the beach
She is definitely a cloud being happy
That's what they do in California
The rain beats the windshield
Because it was a cloud
My daughter chews a cucumber too loud
So I can't hear if the rain will end
A football slices the air like a knife through a watermelon
I was tricked into thinking the day is full of decisions (which was a cloud? what
               was the air?)
A seagull goes crashing
      right into a cloud
because it wants to be a cloud
Hear the waves waking up
from deep sleep says daughter
who was being the clouds so hard
          she and the clouds begin to cry
It's not the place that seems dangerous
      or its clouds
but its people
who walk
fitfully through air
The clouds being hills once hug the hills close

We try blowing but they don't budge
They are stubborn
        unorogenic
California clouds
creating disasters
of the ordinary mind
in their everyday cloud-like way
Every cloud was once a hometown to someone happy   My sobbing
demoiselle
        may turn her tears   beating the clouds
to it   precipitating loads of happy, grief to green
What we can't beat we be

THE WIND IS a thing I'm reckoning with.
In the morning the trees bend for the breeze.

To make yourself happy be like the trees.

But the live oak, you say, stays stiff, and
So it does, under its dress of Spanish moss—so
I guess you'll have to decide which tree to be like.

Anyway   as I'm sitting here in the morning watching I
Can't make anything happen. "World, world, come to
Me," I say, but world won't listen. Not even the birds
Who are something to hear, fuzzing the air with their various
Urgencies: "Listen up! I'm over here on this branch!"
And to the human ear that fought the wind it's
The morning's sweet word even if the bird
Is saying to its neighbor, "Shut the fuck up, Motherfucker."

I FOUND MYSELF in Texas with the buntings, a woman who could no longer perceive human motion. All bodies frozen on the horizon, and there were many. Name it *akinesthesia* or name it *oceanless*. The only thing left is the wind and an emoticon paling at an outer ambit.

If a hundred people donate a dollar, all our transfer events could have to do with money. Don't be frightened THIS IS ART. I take the hundred one-dollar bills and walk out into the desert toward the dusty hem of earth. Toss them into the air. Whosoever finds a dollar will be given a bunting if they sing their story. Dimpsy, the rat-tailed Yorkie on Austin Street, caught a dollar in her jaws.

Next, we will try composting. Who will donate the first dollars for the compost pile?

In Texas, I imagine a cowboy who keeps good house. He is moving slowly, slowly across the horizon on his horse.

BEAUTY ROLLING AROUND in the dust
                                  an incandescence between what

   wanders around among *coming to be* and *decay*

     it's only human

it's like the children's riddle about the eunuch who threw
                    something at a bat:

     A happiness that is not happy throws a shoe that is not a shoe out the
     window (not a window) toward the moon (not a moon)

     till the echo between moon and not moon made its own mooing called song

so with so many bigs and smalls and lights and heavies we describe
                    our happy, our pain

Apply these names in accordance with the beasts
    what it enjoys good
    what angers it bad

You are the beast, be
                    Happy

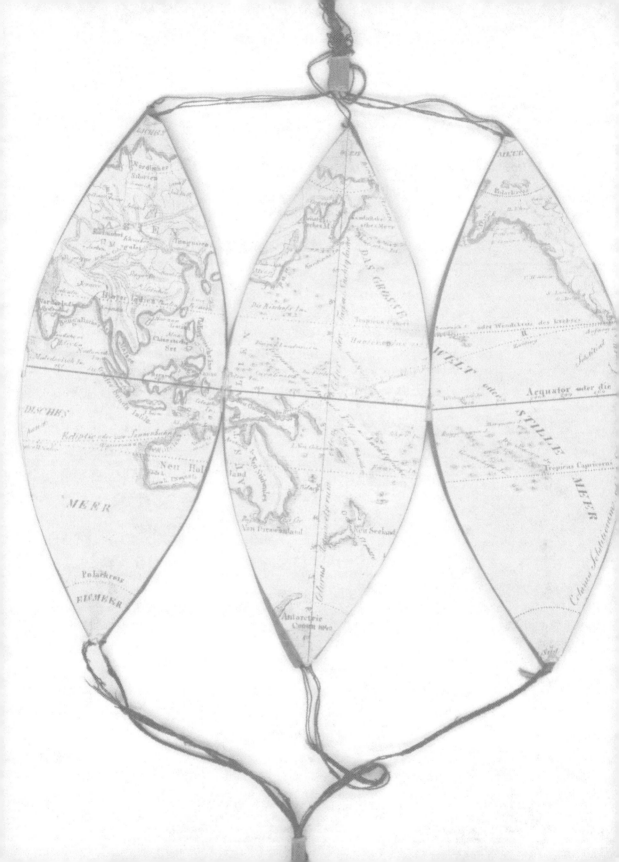

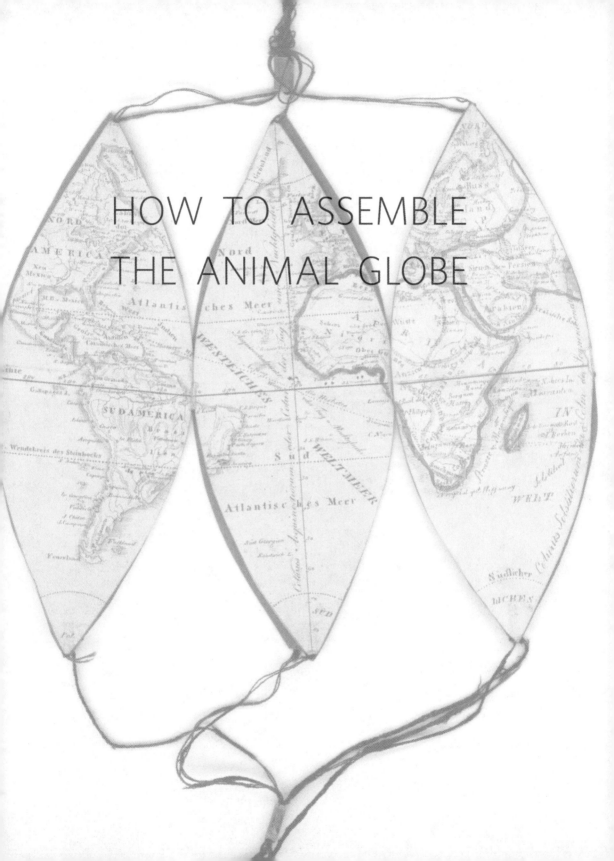

HOW TO ASSEMBLE
THE ANIMAL GLOBE

When an individual is seen gliding through the woods and close to the observer, it passes like a thought, and on trying to see it again, the eye searches in vain, the bird is gone.

AFRICA

BLUEBUCK
(HIPPOTRAGUS LEUCOPHAEUS)
(EX circa 1800)

its blue
        hue
beckoned
            to which side
of blue
it had to drink daily
which made it easy   (to shoot)
        eating the best
red grass, spear grass, love grass
blue from dark skin showing thru

If you travel to Uppsala, Capetown or London you might glimpse one
of the three remaining pairs of horns
A skull in Glasgow, one in Amsterdam
The four mounted specimens (Vienna, Stockholm, Paris, Leiden)
show no sheen of blue

CAPE SERVAL
(LEPTAILURUS SERVAL SERVAL)
(subspecies, thought EX circa 19th or 20th c.)

The cat of spare parts[1]
leaps five feet into the air and can change directions there, snatch a bird
in flight (which, if fowl, it will pluck), hear a mouse
underground, hunt
without seeing its prey

Pounces—40% effective by day
59% in the night

BUBAL HARTEBEEST
(ALCELAPHUS BUSELAPHUS BUSELAPHUS)
(nominate subspecies, North Africa, EX 1925?)

As old as Aeschylus, as old as Hebrew and Pliny
"colour uniform pale rufous or fawn," food to many
 "a frequent inhabitant of menageries"   this
                                          side of the blue
"But we have seen no skin or skull
of a wild-killed specimen";
when viewed head-on, the horns
formed a U; the last captive female

died November 9, Jardin des Plantes, 1923

Get up, you can see that the people have not respected you, get up and walk away

sings the hartebeest, according
to oral tradition

QUAGGA
(EQUUS QUAGGA QUAGGA)
(EX 1870s)

Not a zorse, a zeedonk or a zonkey, though there was once a quorse.
"The only quagga to be photographed alive" was a mare at St. Regent's Park zoo.

ISLANDS

ALDABRA BRUSH WARBLER
(NESILLAS ALDABRANA)
(confirmed EX 1986)

"discovered" in 1967
described in 1968*
lost in 1969
found in 1975†
gone in 1983‡

* based on one nest with a mated pair and three eggs
† six individuals, all males
‡ last known male expired

SHANTY OR CHORUS

The rat and the cat on Tenerife
The pig and the macaque on Mauritius
The dog the cat and the rat
The cat on Acsension
The mongoose, Hawaii
The humans the humans the humans
The rat the cat and the goat on Aldabra, Seychelles
The goat, the feral goat on Pinta, Galápagos
What will they eat? Bird eggs with bread and butter!
What will we eat? Bird eggs what catches the hunter!

MAURITIUS BLUE PIGEON
(ALECTROENAS NITIDISSIMA)
(EX early 1830s)

The Prince of Orange had one in his menagerie
(for a few months) in 1790, and from this we know
the voice: "a dove-like cooing during the day,
and rows of 10–12 *baf* calls in the night"

Did it look like the Dutch
flag or the French? An argument ensued—
Tricolore: head white, tail red, middle blue

It was not, like the pink pigeon (still surviving)
seasonally poisonous or inedible
A *Mauritius Blue* was meat
for escaped slaves, lost sailors

In 1801, the ship *Géographe*'s
chief drawer (assigned maps and birds) was able to get several for roasting[2]
up in the river gorges, saw
the plucked earth coming

STELLER'S SEA COW
(HYDRODAMALIS GIGAS)
(first seen by Europeans near Bering Island in 1741, EX by 1768)

By night, lava-spirits took to the skies to hunt & returned
with a whale impaled on each enormous finger   Volcanoes
lit up for the roasting   Captain Vitus Bering
landed, scurvied, in a storm   then died   As to his shipmates
the meat of the giant sea cow kept them alive

It "drifted just below the surface of the water; a single animal
resembled an overturned boat," and they stripped its skin
for barks

The last cow was killed for its excellent meat
Had they been mistaken for sirens would the flesh have been[3]
so sweet—

Sappho said *Someone will remember us*
to be remembered means what

                            if poetry is
                  la mémoire de la langue
        the sensory remnant, as if we could still taste it on our tongues

when self-making stops
ops (Gr., *eye*) turns wine-dark, into itself
as if twisted in the mirror
εἴδω, I see
eidolons, the ghosts

              Everywhere, worlds touch

ASIA

HOKKAIDŌ AND HONSHŪ WOLVES
(CANIS LUPUS HATTAI AND CANIS LUPUS HODOPHILAX)
(Japan, EX 1889, 1905)

What if your ancestors were raised by wolves
      your relations, wolf spirits
The first known wolf-bounty was five silver *drachmes*
for a male, one for a female (Solon
          got that ratio wrong)
In Dark Ages England, King Æthelstan of the Anglo-Saxons
            demanded
300 wolf pelts each year from King Hywel Dda

Or, if you were a criminal, your penance might be to provide wolf tongues

Mary, Queen of Scots, loved to hunt them in the Atholl Forest
There exist in France today *lieutenants de la louveterie* (Royal Wolfcatchers)
      who keep track of hunting laws and rats
The Honshū wolf was the world's smallest—little bigger than a breadbox
The islanders praised them for keeping crop-eating animals in check
Rabies did them in and strychnine did the Hokkaidō wolf

CRYPTOZOOLOGY

Poetry runs on gossip, why can't animals? Phantom[4]
cats (black

        panthers and pumas way out of their ranges)
Honshū and Hokkaidō wolves heard howling—breathing—stepping on leaves—

I once saw a white detonation from a telephone wire along the highway near
High Falls, N Y—a *symbolon* bursting in the eye—
It was a large raptor, not a speck of rufous/gray seemed to fleck it
Found something close in a bird book—a Gyrfalcon, Old Norse
in name, circling far from its range (the light-colored Gyrfalcons
are found in Greenland, aiding

    crypsis)
    (= ability to self-conceal: nocturnality, transparency, camouflage and mimicry)
    cryptid
    (how deep do you hide?)

A Gyrfalcon
Lays a golden egg
Wing chord, tarsal, tail and culmen working together for
Swan hunting in China

A man with a Gyrfalcon on his fist
Is rich
A woman
With a Gyrfalcon on her mind is
Changing the yaw angle midflight

BAIJI
(LIPOTES VEXILLIFER)
(First described in the Erya, 3 BCE, last [unconfirmed] sighting 2007)[5]

Goddess of the Yangtze
Left-behind flag bearer
A princess thrown to the river by her father for following
      her own counsel
The first Laowai who saw one shot it, shipped it
to the Smithsonian

      "You approach your refined language" and then you
          move away

BLACK SOFTSHELL TURTLE
(NILSSONIA NIGRICANS)
(EX 2002)[6]

each turtle
a sinner
saved by a saint
the last party
of saved sinners lives
in a pond by the Chittagong shrine

JAPANESE RIVER OTTER
(LUTRA LUTRA WHITELEYI)
(last sighted 1979, declared EX 2012)

It ate
eels,
beetles,
crabs, shrimp,
fish,
watermelon and
sweet potatoes

ARABIAN OSTRICH
(STRUTHIO CAMELUS SYRIACUS)
(subspecies; last verified individual shot and eaten by pipeline workers, 1941, near Jubail[7])

If you had a team of them
drawing your chariot, you would seem
to be
         flying

But the bird
forgot to praise Allah and came
    crashing down, sun-
singed

Were you a pharaoh, you'd be
fanned
by its feathers

My people is become cruel like the ostriches in the wilderness
                                        —Lamentations 4:3; yet

they are ever at their eggs, the female by day, the male
by night, in
millenary repose as

al-Jahiz painted it

ENTHEOGEN (CHORUS)

It's the ghost dance of all the animals

beating earth
w/ their hooves

it's the black crow dance of reality

P U R G E

the who-me bubble
out front
golden   popping who-me bubble

Reality keeps throwing up
her circus tents

plays a little
song on the
harmonica
to accompany herself out
swish swish

Reality's really
dirty
even its roosters
are making me
laugh

Everybody's hoarding
Everybody's barfing up
the world's extra energy

Throwing up reality

So the animals' ghost dance is
what we get

They will never be done Never be
done dancing   If we wipe them
from the face of the earth
they will never be done being
part of it   making the world with their
sounds & feet & hooves

until they are done dancing the
animals' ghost dance &
then they will be done

AMERICAS

ECTOPISTES MIGRATORIUS
(EX 1914)

The dung fell in spots, not unlike melting flakes of snow; and the continued buzz of wings
had a tendency to lull my senses to repose[8]

Slave-meat, hog-meat
that cheap
Sent more than a million pigeons to market from one roost
Trap: sew a pigeon's eyes shut and let it cry, others will come
from flocks so great they topple trees

In air, their massing backs a
                         glistening sheet
      of azure iridesce   *and anon,* at a turn
suddenly—*a rich deep purple*

In Kentucky, townsfolk talked and ate nothing but Pigeon for a week
Even the air smelled of it

Of their courtship: "the tenderness and affection
displayed by these birds towards their mates are in the highest
degree striking" (see *two birds billing*), their love song a
monosyllabled string: *coo-coo-coo-coo, kee-kee-kee-kee,* the first
note the loudest, like a bell diminishing

CHILE DARWIN'S FROG
(RHINODERMA RUFUM)
(no confirmed sightings since 1978)

The male
lifted the embryos up and
stored them
in his voice

EL SOLITARIO JORGE
(CHELONOIDIS NIGRA ABINGDONII)

—Lonesome George at Charles Darwin Research Station

—Lonesome George with His Female Companions (not his type)

—Lonesome George Becomes Unexpectedly Amorous (no luck with the eggs)

—Lonesome George Dead at 100

—The last of his 10,000,000-year-old line[10]

RED-BELLIED GRACILE MOUSE OPOSSUM OR COMADREJITA DE VIENTRE ROJO
(CRYPTONANUS IGNITES)
(Jujuy province, Argentina; last seen in 1962; Small Nonvolant Mammals Red List)

The entire area where the type specimen was collected has been converted to
agriculture and industry [steel mills] and extensive searches over the last 44
years have failed to locate [it]

Nothing is known about the natural history of this species

—Assessors M. Diaz & R . Barquez

.

Small fiery fairy gracile

I have said much of your bad possum cousins to the north

I was ungracious

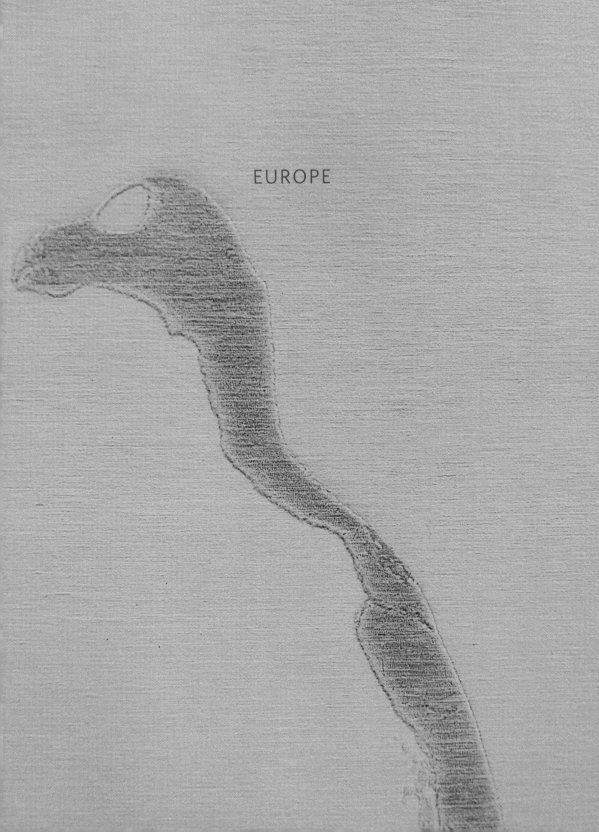

EUROPE

AUROCHS
(BOS PRIMIGENIUS)
(last female died in the Jaktorów Forest, 1627, after 400,000 years of evolution)

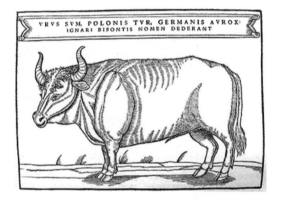

I am urus, tur in Polish, aurox in German, dunces
call me bison

—Sigismund von Herberstein, 1556

battle beast to the Romans
vast, swift, fast, dangerous, your
hamburger's ancestor

the last aurochs skull (huge, to carry all that horn) stolen
by the Swedish army (circa 1665) (now you can see it
in the Stockholm Royal Armory)

boy-calves a chestnut color changing to deep
brown; down
the spine:
a white
eel-
stripe

(for mixing up the predators' eyes)

PYRENEAN IBEX
(CAPRA PYRENAICA PYRENAICA)
(EX 2000)[11]

to graze in
winter in snow-
free meadows

PIED RAVEN
(CORVUS CORAX VARIUS MORPHA LEUCOPHAEUS)[12]
(last seen 1948)

Every Faroe male of hunting age…to shoot…one raven…per year or
be fined four skillings

over hill and dale   the only thing moving
like a riddle a raven
is as little in its yellow eye
as mine

GREAT AUK
(PINGUINUS IMPENNIS)
(last known breeding pair 1844, last sighting 1852)

Three Icelandic fishermen saw the last known nesting pair;
 killed them both and crushed their egg

"a beautiful bird of bizarre proportions"

cooked them live in a burning pot
over other burning auks
 "their bodys being oily soon produce a Flame"

to be buried with auk bones,
covered in auk beaks, to be wrapped in an auk-skin cloak

auction off this severe unction undoing the glue sinew by sinew, sell it
to whom

it may concern
you

to never see
a living auk
severed

AUSTRALIA/OCEANIA

TASMANIAN TIGER
(THYLACINUS CYNOCEPHALUS)
(Dog-headed pouched one; last captive animal died, Hobart Zoo, 1936)

"Hidden away in a Sydney vault is a young, pickled pup"

looks like a dog

stripes like a tiger

carries its young like a kangaroo

Abel Tasman saw in 1642 tracks on the shore of "wild beasts having claws like a *Tyger*"

This carnivorous marsupial liked the same midland, woodland and coastal heath as did

the British settlers

LORD HOWE GERYGONE
(GERYGONE INSULARIS)
(no records of the species since 1928, when it was heard, not seen; none seen or heard since 1936)[13]

pale gray eye-ring rising

eye to ear

the feathers like its fathers' leading

to its eyebrows

gray throat and chin

with the back of its head

leading to its tail

with the tip of its tail

pointing past the horizon

the portion of its body lining the rib cage

under the feathers, the pink skin

inside the rib cage, the simmering heart

a yellow fairy-blown thumbprint at the chin, breast pale gray

down the belly, a softened sunsplash

The Lord Howe Gerygone had pink eggs, eyes that matched

The Lord Howe Gerygone gone, gone on

not much to look at, but

"born of sound"

it sang in canopies of trees a song like "Pop-Goes-the-Weasel"

and noisy after the rains

the hood of its nest

hung by spiderweb from the tip of a twig wing

twing

DUSKY FLYING FOX
(PTEROPUS BRUNNEUS)[14]
(EX 1874?)

Little red flying fox
Black box flying fox
Gray-headed flying fox
Spectacled flying fox
Look the lack of
Dusky flying fox

Flying foxes drinking
Flying foxes dancing
Flying foxes gathering in trees
Flying foxes thinking
About Dusky
Flying fox; zero among the leaves

Spectacled flying foxes favor eucalypt blossom nectar
Black flying fox hanging in a bottlebrush tree recording pollen data
          in the cockpit of its brain
Gray-headed flying foxes singing with their milk teeth and later stealing mangoes
Little red flying fox's larynx-box squawking like a scared screen-door spring

Advice from the experts: *Their droppings won't strip paint from cars*
                    but don't leave your washing on the line overnight

Flying foxes make the sound of a skater's blade striking ice as they skim the lake
With their bellyfur full of water
Dew-licking leaves

FOR YOU TO WRITE ABOUT

Broad-faced Potoroo
Darling Downs Hopping Mouse
Crescent Nail-tail Wallaby
Pig-footed Bandicoot

       Mysterious Starling
       Society Parakeet
       Tonga Ground Skink
       Sea Mink

Mogollon Mountain Wolf
Bali Tiger
Turgid-blossom Pearly Mussel
Javan Tiger
Atitlán Grebe

       24-rayed Sunstar (*Heliaster solaris*—disappeared during
          the El Niño Southern Oscillation in the early '80s)
       Dusky Seaside Sparrow
       Caspian Tiger
       Formosan Clouded Leopard

St. Croix Racer
Western Black Rhino
Bermudan Saw-whet Owl
Platypus Frog

Atlas Bear (used for sport in Roman Empire, the last one shot c. 1879)
California Grizzly
Darwin's Rice Rat
Cry Pansy (the only plant I will include)
Indefatigable Galápagos Mouse (Muse)

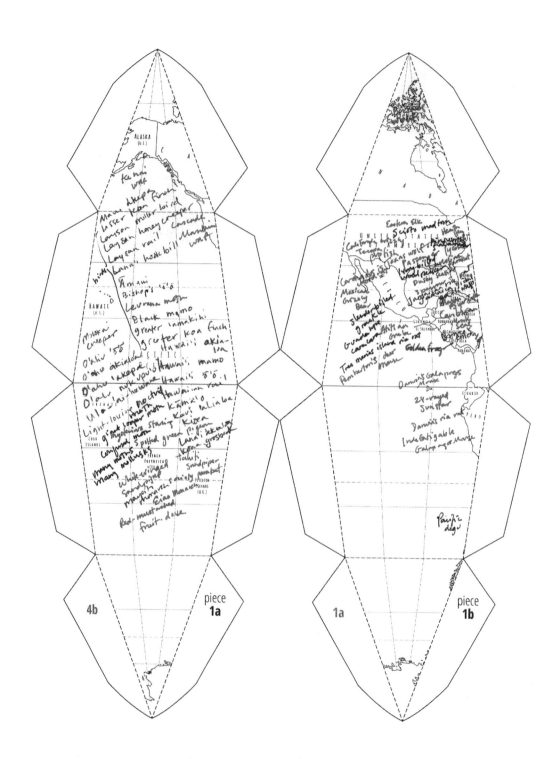

ALASKA
(U.S.)

Kenai
Wolf
Maui deepa
lesser Koa Finch
Lesser miller-bird
Laysan honeycreeper
Laysan rail Cascade
Lāna'i hookbill wolf

HAWAI'I
(U.S.)

'Āmaui
Bishop's 'ō'ō
Laysan moth
Black mamo
greater 'amakihi
greater koa finch
Hawai'i 'akia-
pōlā'au
Hawai'i mamo
Hawai'i 'ō'ū
Hawai'i rail
Kaua'i 'akialoa
Kaua'i nukupu'u
Lāna'i 'ake'ake'a
Kona grosbeak

Moloka'i
creeper
O'ahu 'ō'ō
O'ahu 'akialoa
O'ahu 'akepa
O'ahu nukupu'u
O'ili'ili'ai honna
Ula-'ai-hawane moth
light-louise moth
giant looper moth
Thysdraus staini
conifond moth
many moths spotted green Pigeon
many mollusks

Tahiti
sandpiper

FRENCH
POLYNESIA
White-willigid
sandpiper
Marsh
Eiao
Red-moustached
fruit-dove

Marquesan society parakeet
MARQUESAS
ISLANDS
(U.S.)

COOK
ISLANDS

4b

piece
1a

CANADA

UNITED STATES
Eastern elk
Scioto mud turtle
California's bobl ...
Texas Herb ...
Texas wolf ...
cliff fish
Passeng ...
... bird
Wood rat ...
Dusky ...
... wolf

Coronado Isl
Mexican
Grizzly
Bear

Slender-billed
Jackrabbit
Guadalupe
caracara
Tree mouse island rice rat
Pemberton's deer mouse

GUATEMALA
EL SALVADOR
NICARAGUA

CUBA JAMAICA
HAITI

Ahll'an
Grebe
Golden Frog

PANAMA

Darwin's Gala pagos
mouse

24-rayed
Sun star

ECUADOR

PERU
Darwin's rice rat
Indefatigable
Galapagos Mouse

Pacific
degu

1a

piece
1b

LOST AND FOUND (LAZARUS SPECIES)

Miller's Grizzled Langur
Leadbeater's Possum*
Philippine Bare-backed Fruit Bat
Monito del Monte[†]
Chacoan Peccary
Giant "Albino" Earthworm[‡]
La Palma Giant Lizard
Laotian Rock Rat (its meat found at market)
Bermuda Petrel
Majorcan Midwife Toad
Takahe[§]
Black Kokanee
Cuban Solenodon (mammal with a venomous bite)
Lord Howe Island Stick Insect**
New Caledonian Crested Gecko (found again after a 1994 storm)
Coelacanth (thought dead 65 million years)

* matriarchal, living in upper canopy of world's tallest trees
† like a few other animals on this list, thought to have gone extinct 11 million years ago
‡ Palouse earthworm, 3.3 feet long, found in Idaho and Washington; said to smell like lilies
§ flightless bird, last four specimen taken 1898, discovered again 1948, Lake Anau, NZ
** aka walking sausage or land lobster, thought gone in 1920; around 24 individuals found under one shrub
   on a sea stack in 2001

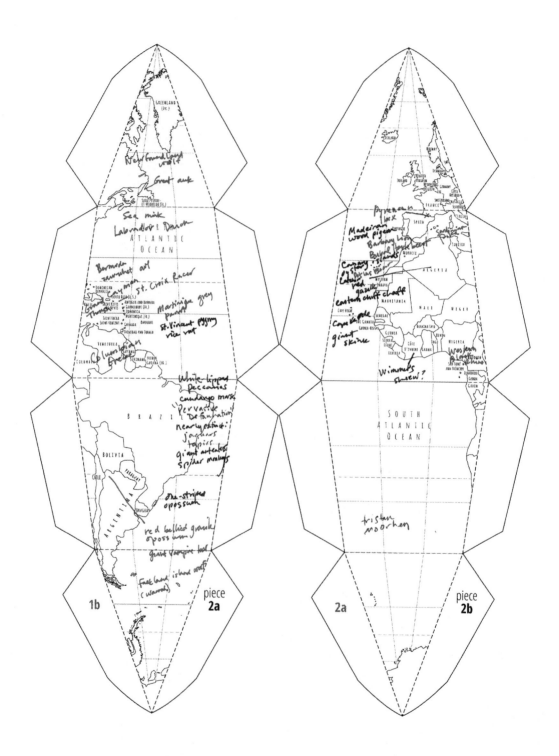

piece
1b

piece
2a

2a

piece
2b

ANTARCTICA

Ice

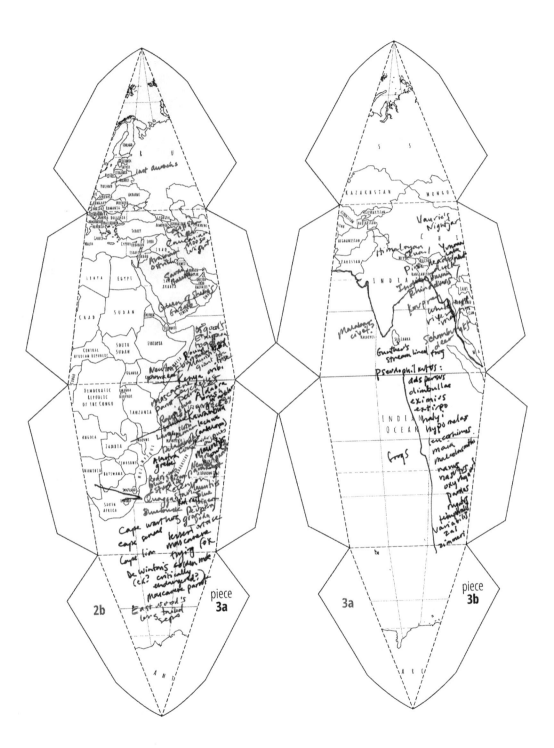

NOT-ENTHEOGEN (ANTISTROPHE)

We all began to think about the end
Of the world. We thought
We would
Kill
All the Animals.
A kind of regret
Began to nuzzle in at
The back of the neck
'S brain.
It was voluptuous
Our hands sanding the
Curving body, we could say
At a dinner party, We've
Almost Killed
All the Animals,
Regretfully, we could
All agree it was
More than that, we were
Terrible. We were
Comforted
By our horror, drapey
And powerful, loose folds
Over the body, we could
Swathe it over the furniture, a leaky surface we could
Almost touch. Infinity is
Soft-bodied, we liked

To discover new disasters because
It is not us
Dying out by the
Train of
Burnt
Out stars.
   Of the world we're
Not that powerful. What
Is "world"? There is
No end to it.

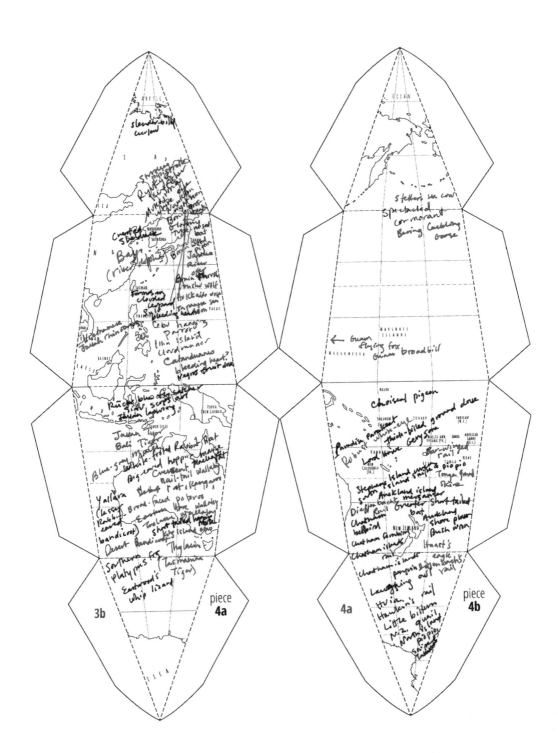

Piece 4a (left globe gore)

ARCTIC O.

slender-billed curlew

Steller's
Ryukyu
Miyako
Bonin
Crested Shelduck
Bajji
(river dolphin)
Bonin
Japanese River Otter
Formosan clouded leopard
Hokkaido wolf
Formosan sea
bleeding heart
Cebu hanging Parrot
Ilin Island Cloud runner
Catanduanes bleeding heart?
Negros fruit dove
blue-eyed
Ründu? scops owl
Hidden lapwing
Javan tiger
Bali Tiger
Blue-gray Mouse
White-footed Rabbit Rat
Pig-rooted hopping mouse
Crescent Nailtail
Rail-tail Wallaby
Yallara (Lesser Rabbit eared bandicoot)
Stick-nest rat Kangaroo
Broad-faced potoroo
Eastern Hare Wallaby
Toolache wallaby
Desert Bandicoot
Short-tailed hopping
Lesser Island emu
Southern platypus frog
Thylacine (Tasmanian Tiger)
Eastwood's whip lizard

3b   piece **4a**

Piece 4b (right globe gore)

S. OCEAN

Steller's sea cow
Spectacled cormorant
Bering Cackling Goose

MARSHALL ISLANDS
Guam flying fox
Guam broadbill
MICRONESIA

NAURU
Choiseul pigeon
SOLOMON IS. TUVALU TOKELAU (N.Z.)
Paradise Parrot eye
Robust white-eye
Thick-billed ground dove
WALLIS AND FUTUNA (Fr.) SAMOA AMERICAN SAMOA (U.S.)
Lord Howe Gerygone
NEW CALEDONIA (Fr.) FIJI TONGA NIUE NEW
Bar-winged rail
Po'ouli
Stephens Island wren
Tonga Ground
Bush-island snipe Skink
Auckland Island Shore
Dieffenbach's Rail
Chatham bock merganser
Greater Short-tailed bat
Auckland Island Shore plover
Chatham bellbird
Chatham Gambier
Bush wren
Chatham island rail
Chatham island
Chatham-island
Haast's eagle
penguin Dieffenbach's rail
Laughing owl
Huia
Hawkins's rail
Little bittern
N.Z. quail
Po'ouli
NEW ZEALAND

4a   piece **4b**

It was then that the authors of all this devastation began their entry amongst the dead, the dying, and the mangled. The pigeons were picked up and piled in heaps, until each had as many as he could possibly dispose of, when the hogs were let loose to feed on the remainder.

ORACLE OR, UTOPIA

NO ONE KNOWS how it began.
A few atoms lying in the sun
began to lick and burn.
Then, man.

Human human burning bright
In the fistlings of the night

Hatching what in the watery den

Morning was the first hour's other side
Pink and orange paling up the scaffold
Soon, we could see a few cities from the roof

Earth—if it can be glimpsed at all—is a flicker of tiny lights

．

outside her head
a boy ignites the snow with his red shovel
he digs and digs again
making the wingspan grow
there is an easy essay in it: what it
means to be live alive.
when the world made its first sounds
the large-nerved meganeura flew
at the roof of the world. what it means
to be gone agone

First the wings were 2.5 feet wide—300
million years later it was
a thumb-lengthed dragon fly

.

hearing the houses of their small white voices
    vibrating inside the dome
  the crisp "t" of the color moving against its walls
      as if the "t" were a tongue & the walls were its mouth

    as if the vowel were a mouth and the world was its mother
the consonants licking the tin clean

    as if the "t" were a time-scrap banging into distant water towers

The South Lung hangs to the left

In the rainforest basement
we patience our Oracle

Filled the aquifer with 700,000 gallons of water brought in on milk trucks
then mixed it with Instant Ocean

step inside the North Lung when the day gets long
hear the Hypalon expand and pull
16 tons

White-spaced dome the white air whistles through
What skins left to throw
over the structures   Nights we show
        holographic bats   wild cats   on translucent walls

in the Animal Theater, we hunt or cuddle them
flesh-eye-to-false-eye
        membranes the real

Mornings, we stitch up breathing tarps
in case the Big Lung unseams

They took the city & its human beings
        but first they
                wiped it clean

·

When I had taken the long way home I was looking
For something   What   I had not lost it for I had not found it
A Damselfly a Darner A Truth
About how we came to be
Lying here by the side of the brown river by the side of the road

You put your
Right foot into
Your right shoe because
This is what you do
To keep your foot from
Glass and goatweed This is
How to live

•

How to live a thousand years,
unragging our telomeres, then

go quiet.

•

I was down in that dark pit
when it was completely empty

Down in the ditch licking the dark
You can't live in this wind

so climb out of the pit

probing milliseconds for
microscopic black holes in the Tevatron

though such a thing has yet to be seen in nature

how we came to be
non-vanishing masses
in the future

how we came to be
symmetry-breaking

[rocks
faces]

We built our fog desert,   paludarium   mangrove wetland above
the technosphere—hear it
rattle and moan
in pipes below
our feet—

above, built the glass roofs too low
for *Trochilidae*, and bees can't read
vitrine, so cockroaches and ants pollinate

night, we hear the bush-babies'
clucking chuckling croaking babylike cries—

anywhere on Erthe—in the dark—when the plants rest— CO_2
fluctuates, O_2
goes low, so
Doc gives us nocturnal   shining   oxygen shots

how to do stress wood without
the tiniest breeze (where the tree's flesh responds
to wind, or snow, gravity, and ground-shifts,   goes tough
and keeps the tree up) in the vivarium?

stress word shift this   this

some crows lost their caw
their predator warning
(their predators were gone)
we lost some vowels
down in the bowels, the organ-chambers where meaning
rounds itself toward night, a light

.

in the inner-space experiment   J says   disorder reflects
the chaos from the beginning
          every time a glass breaks   every time a Russian grips, tries
to drag her off-camera for a kiss

----

    you cannot heave the whole thing backwards

Do not fry a man
to make yourself happy. What
does the State? Tell it
to wait, wait
for

I am dreaming of my daughter's old roller skates.
The metal of them smashed into days.

How came we to be
symmetry-breaking

     death   luck
   happiness   greed

                  we were like
half the goddess's face as ash-color
like the corpse, half blue-black
where the blood collects

make the sides of color come together, licking the stitches of blue
       as if the consonant were its black
          and the vowels were its white   We can

bring them back
together, *idaltu*

we know this because in the future we can peek through the body-window and
see the corpse.
        the
dead inside the living. our mitochondrial
Eve. In the Laboratory of Artificial
Anatomy, we work
the living inside the dead. the wood and strings. it's a bit of
flame folded up in the organs like a love

letter inside a drunk man's
pocket. All we need is
when to spark it.

■

because we had everything in common except our bodies
what sightless city on the horizon we knew how to grow
(stretch the stem cells over the scaffolds)

body (girl) you led me astray

when we have our bodies in common
livers cropped together in one cornfield,
             the *tuh* and the *unh*
         the *feather* and *father* of our noises
             herded in one mouth
we will build it beautiful

it is our city and we
are its dogs

■

its lawful honey-colored
girls & boys using

the words in

unison: my

wave by which the gold plains of space
break

As if the roof
        Were a reef

*

Anything we cannot grow or make, we dig for
We dig a hole in the ground
We are hole-diggers
we dig and we dig

shirred
aggregates
mineral iridium
irresidue
smacked us Come
smacked us Come
the reactor
Nuclear
Heart atom
o come

.

time-mongrels devour the stray hours
cleaning up a crooked calendar
gnawing stray days off a dogged edge

cats nibbling minutes like
gnawing at a flea   Bite
          time's body before   it bites   you

     become then
          we become again

     until we are become   [undone

          ▪

We come round again   stitched up at the sound

          ▪

Queen   of   a   syntax
When I return you to Earth
                        you'll speak
with water on your tongue, yr tongue
        been drilling
                    a waterless planet

        well well

we speak that language here

    .

the last mad grasshoppers leaping wildly crossways
            from the snow
    "quanta does flow"
It goes on without you

    .

[what can no longer be held in language]
[sieve]
[sieve]
[where does the future take place]
[words were sent through the collider]
[letters atomize, chinks in the particles]
[water is not money]
[wht is not money]
[pouring through]
[the ey/e fell apart from its word]
[then the m   then the   o]
[it does not accelerate]
[does it]
[i agination   ny]
[it slows and]
[accelerates]

[do a biosphere]
[do a new biosphere]
[do a new]
[money word]
[worldview]
[your like-body][(*līc*-shape)]   [Old English: *body*]
feorhbold, feorhhold   [O E: *body, body*]

you were once
fear-hold
        feather-bold
                father
going *earsgang* first   [*arse*]
till shape shook out your creature
with the many words for *face*   [*ondwlita, onsīen*]

·

she was having her language hold money
        I don't want any money in my language I said
Imagination money

P U R G E

·

        put the originals
namely, the animals around us,   all the plants
back into time   (somewhere for safekeeping)
(we had taken them out)
(first the animals disappeared, their sounds, then their names)
we had forgotten their faces
their faces are not our faces

so the likeness is to the thing that it is like   I like   like
having lions around

onli lions can lie here
on this part of other Erthe

our last zebra   *Hypertext transfer Not found*

our last long-fingered frog   *Hypertext transfer Not found*

our last fruit bat   *Hypertext transfer*

our last angel shark   *Not Found Not Found*

put them in the oracle

                        shark   h ark   ark

put them in the leaky coracle

put the letters in the tin can and rattle them around

----

angel-sounds like a loud shark

----

gathering up the atoms to find a woman who rhymes with time
to find all the letters in the t

                g r r

Sun was a power
an overflapping treasury we tapped

That's a short time you're talking about!
It's nothing compared to the whole of time.

        Isn't that so?
It is.
Then, if the past
     comes busting in like a band of cocked revolvers
          takes the color *apple-pale* out of sound
          and arguing about human beings
          takes the *you* out of future
          fture [words] out of *līc*-shape
              scarring across the language
          and puts the thing back in their things
          how say

        What do you mean?

The Sun is not sight but is seen
That's right.
The words are not things but they mean.
Not true.
Find a sound as resilient and rigid as a flight-feather.
Break open the words and shake out all their money.

They sought to erase from my face
all evidence
that I had lived

They used needles to do it. Extraction methods and plumping.

Ocean makes a slurry sound behind my head
a   o   sound

       It was silent as the atoms were gathering
       Then it got noisy

       Sound made the ocean make sound &

We found history on the Earth's wrinkled face

   ▪

seen a woman who rhymed with time

does her decay
       does her primordial radionuclide dress
and its disintegrating daughters
do time

   ▪

when you peel off your dead skin to see the face of the world
      the already-dead go deathly pale
self is a god we walked through   I was an idiot It was a mistake
I believe something here
       What self?
I do not believe the man-made sky
       I think like a hero
       I think like a dog
I was looking for the real sky
I want more face, more mother
more atoms moving through the heart
       Get ready
I am taking man back for woman, mankind

wanted
to make no rupture here
only continuity
to watch not the still-shot but
all the pictures moving forward and back
the old rock dust and the new new planet
each canyon or gulley, "the side of the smooth green hill, torn

by floods…a gash on a living animal" scabbed over, ornamented

by time   for which there is no gracious
synonym
mynonys
symmetry
mnemosyne if poetry is
the memory of language   rupture   go
tonguing

        rapture

the tones came back after they had wiped the surface
of the vowels in circular motion

     at some remote point in that past people
had hands and fathers   we agree

do I even know where I am?
Is there anything out there? The letters are falling through air
They started with feathers, then iron and hands

If I could pull a skillet from your face   make it
     full of food
  to give away   put time right

I look up at the sky,   scan
   for atoms,   colors,   vowels

It's a watercolor in knots
There are quite a few things breaking

sound stops I   –

                                      –   –

                                   –   –

              use word-waste to build it, Oracle   –

                                       –

spine lost its e   might lost it y   for lost its m at th nd of tim
spin th carousl round
          again

shirrd
aggrgats
minral iridium
irrsidu
smackd us Com
smackd us Com
th ractor
Nuclar
Hart atom
o com

                    at th nd of tm
spn th carousl round
          agan

smckd s Cm
smckd s Cm
th rctr
Nclr
Hrt tm
cm

EPODE

Is there a river here? Does it intersect the city?
Is there a sea? Roads winding away
toward the Dalles and self-
storage lots. Are we headed north?
Are we near the capitol? The
battlements lit up in neon &
the damp stank of underbridge struts.
A sign says "Form" and
nothing else.   And suddenly
from the shadowed outskirts we burst into the circle
of lights, away from Ikea & all
that unwinds itself by night. Surge & richness

depth   hardiness   color   air
touching
its mouth to all
of us

When you say Us you mean Earth's

sounds & tint, spikes & curve,
    each liquid shape   our very
wilds—

    A band rumbles
brightly at the corner, a crowd percolates, someone
has cleared the glitter-
trash off stage. You
are alive and in
a little shiver between cause & attentiveness, clockwise, counter-, Joy

shouts itself

THERE WERE ANCIENT QUESTIONS INSIDE MY HEAD (RIDER)

When I was seven, two Chilean scientists introduced *autopoiesis* to say how living beings produce themselves ceaselessly. A cell, for example, is an auto-poietic entity: it is self-producing and autonomous, yet connected to its larger environment. It might profoundly change its identity in the course of its life, through interaction with its surroundings, but still manages to be itself. At some point, that possibility will collapse; until then, producer is product, autonomous, self-circulating, and also borrows things from around itself to make itself. The foot is always adjusting to the shoe, and the shoe in kind stretches to fit the foot.

"So the distinction between objective / subjective is merely what?" asked one.

Then the foot is attached to an ankle, and so on.

Somewhere, worlds touch.

First we gave language to the body, comparing it to nests and snakes

Then language began to be evacuated of the body shapes

We lost words for face

But poets know *poiesis* is *to make*

As is *facere,* which is also *to face*

To make a face

A face (a form) (shared root)

To face up to it

To self-make

Face to face

As in a mirror

To eye

To see

Tongue Tooth Neck Throat

Shoulder Arm Elbow Hand Finger

Thigh Knee Ankle Foot

Toe

Nail

Claw

Wing

Feather

Breast

Udder

Navel

Heart

Liver

To put your antique forehead up against them all

And look

Un-inveigling

What color world is it?

I offer "yellow"   Is it enough?

Happiness

is a form of it (*autopoiesis*) —: is it

recyclable? How many vowels do we need to mean it? What is the waste at the
end of use?

Hppnss: "even if everyone exchanged germs

[it's] only for amateurs," said C. D. Wright

In the old country, too, they studied up on how to live, hoping to reach
the necropolis in joy, and invented words like *eudaimonia* to speak of it:
"flourishing," "good spirit," the good composed of all goods, resources
sufficient for a living creature

　　　　a righteous guiding inner d(a)emon, against all the noiseless back-
ground computing occurring even as you sleep

And so you sport across the edges of earnest pursuit, and find yourself among the amateurs. The centaurs and hybrids; the opposite instances in which a face is wiped out of its features. When did my ambidextrous happiness impinge on amphibians and spell apocalypse. Can we call an amphibian a face?

When amphibians call out their own joie de vivre and the waters turn brackish.

Try a bell jar in the Sonoran desert to see what can survive beyond all happiness.

Of happiness, what have we lost? What wilds it?

My loves

I call all

of you.

Here, I want you entirely happy.

ENDNOTES: HOW TO ASSEMBLE THE ANIMAL GLOBE

1. So-called because it looks like it's made of scraps from various animals: long legs, enormous ears, long neck, small head, back legs longer than the front.

2. Jacques-Gérard Milbert, who wrote in his journal: "Il est un point où . . . le défrichement doit s'arrêter, si l'on ne veut, en peu d'années, voir succéder à un pays verdoyant et fertile, une terre aride et dépouillée."

3. Lonely sailors are said to have mistaken manatees, the sea cow's cousin, for sirens.

4. Human science is also a human story. We gossip around the atoms.

5. To listen to a baiji, go to Discovery of Sound in the Sea: http://www.dosits.org/files /dosits/baiji_whistle.mp3.

6. This species was declared Extinct in the Wild (EW) in 2002, when a small population was living in a pond at the Shrine of Bayazid Bastami in Bangladesh. That population has since been increasing, and several small communities have been found in the wild. When is it safe to move an animal to the Lazarus list?

7. Jubail is now the Middle East's largest petrochemical city.

8. John James Audubon, "Passenger Pigeon," *Birds of America:* "I cannot describe to you the extreme beauty of their evolutions, when a Hawk chanced to press upon the rear of the flock. At once, like a torrent, and with a noise like thunder, they rushed into a compact mass, pressing upon each other towards the centre. In these almost solid masses, they darted forward in undulating and angular lines, descended and swept close over the earth with inconceivable velocity, mounted perpendicularly so as to resemble a vast column, and, when high, were seen wheeling and twisting within their continued lines, which then resembled the coils of a gigantic serpent."

"Suddenly there burst forth a general cry of 'Here they come!' The noise which they made, though yet distant, reminded me of a hard gale at sea passing through the rigging of a close-reefed vessel. . . . I found it quite useless to speak, or even to shout to those persons who were nearest to me. Even the reports of the guns were seldom heard, and I was made aware of the firing only by seeing the shooters reloading."

9. Martha (named for Mrs. Washington), an *endling* (the last of her kind), died solo in the Cincinnati Zoo, September 1, 1914; was frozen into a block of ice and shipped to the Smithsonian; there gutted, skinned, mounted. You can see Martha spin in virtual space: http://vertebrates.si.edu/birds/Martha/index.html.

10. Addendum, 2012: 17 Pinta hybrids were found living at Wolf Volcano, Isabela Island, a living ancestor probably dumped there by sailors or pirates. This is now a Lazarus species.

11. Celia, the last known Pyrenean ibex, was found under a fallen tree with her skull crushed. The last known wild male died in 1991. For some time, there remained 10 known ibexes alive, all female.

    A cryopreservation sample from Celia's ear was used in nuclear transfer, her DNA injected into 439 domestic goat eggs, 57 of these implanted into surrogate goats, resulting in 7 pregnancies, of which resulted one live birth. The infant ibex lived 7 minutes before dying of lung failure.

    http://www.telegraph.co.uk/news/science/science-news/4409958/Extinct-ibex-is-resurrected-by-cloning.html

    http://www.petermaas.nl/extinct-archive/speciesinfo/pyreneanibex.htm

12. A pied raven is a color morph, not necessarily a distinct subspecies, so its genes may simply still be in hiding: http://www.cykelkurt.com/fugle/eng/crows-of-the-world.html.

13. The Lord Howe Gerygone's demise was thought to be brought about by the shipwreck of the SS Makambo, 1918, from which black rats invaded Lord Howe Island, leading also to the destruction of the Lord Howe Fantail, the Lord Howe Island Thrush (the Doctor Bird), the Lord Howe Starling, and the Robust White-eye, as well as 12 invertebrate species. The stick insect listed among the Lazarus species on page 109 was thought to have been wiped out by these black rats, too, but was found on Ball's Pyramid, a volcanic stack, nearly a century later.

http://blogs.scientificamerican.com/running-ponies/lord-howe-island-stick-insects-are-going-home

14. The Percy Island flying fox or Dusky flying fox (*Pteropus brunneus*) "is known from a single specimen collected in 1859 [housed at the British Museum], and described in 1878." There was some dispute about its taxonomy (it is similar to *Pteropus scapulatus*), but it was "validated as a separate species late in the 20th century," long after its ravishing.

http://www.environment.gov.au/node/14640

http://australianmuseum.net.au/Australian-bats

http://www.bellingen.com/flyingfoxes/drinking_in_the_river.htm

http://www.inaturalist.org/taxa/40889-Pteropus-brunneus

■

Other sites accessed in researching animals in *How to Assemble the Animal Globe:*

Francis Harper. *Extinct and Vanishing Mammals of the Old World.* New York: American Committee for International Wild Life Preservation, 1945: http://www.archive.org/stream/extinctvanishing00harprich#page/643/mode/1up.

The IUCN Red List of Threatened Species: http://www.iucnredlist.org.

Lucas Brouwers. "The Last Great Auk." Thoughtomics (blog), accessed May 14, 2016: http://www.lucasbrouwers.nl/blog/2011/03/the-last-great-auk.

Tanya Dewey. "Pinguinus impennis—Great Auk." Animal Diversity Web (ADW), accessed October 4, 2016: http://animaldiversity.org/accounts/Pinguinus_impennis.

Bryan Nelson. "Lazarus Species: 13 'Extinct' Animals Found Alive—Laotian Rock Rat." Mother Nature Network (website), published November 5, 2009: http://www.mnn.com/earth-matters/animals/photos/lazarus-species-13-extinct-animals-found-alive/laotian-rock-rat.

I have used the Linnaean system of naming to identify these species, with some reluctance. We cannot categorize all our relations, and all the scientific ordering in the world won't bring these animals back. These are black holes in the system.

 IMAGES

"Festival of Colors" photograph by Laird Hunt; used with permission.

Gotham Girls Roller Derby video still (from *I Am Not Tame*) by Nancy B. Davidson; used with permission.

Bhutan's Gross National Happiness campaign photograph by Mario Biondi (the writer, not the singer); public domain; see also: http://worldhappiness.report.

The map that opens *How to Assemble the Animal Globe* by Joseph Franz Kaiser, 1840; retrieved from the Library of Congress: https://www.loc.gov/item/2008626530; public domain.

Throughout *How to Assemble the Animal Globe:* Christine Lee's blind embossings; created in collaboration for this book and used with permission.

Bubal Hartebeest photograph by Lewis Medland, 1895, in London Zoo; public domain.

Quagga photograph by Frank Haes, 1864; file from the Biodiversity Heritage Library, contributed by Harvard University, Museum of Comparative Zoology, Ernst Mayr Library; used with kind permission from the Zoologische Staatssammlung Muenchen (Bavarian State Collection of Zoology).

Steller's sea cow illustration by L. Stejneger, c. 1887; file from the Biodiversity Heritage Library, contributed by the MBLWHOI Library; public domain.

Photograph of Martha in her case at the Smithsonian from the Smithsonian Institute Archives, image #SIA2010-0612; public domain.

Aurochs engraving by Sigismund von Herberstein, 1556; public domain.

Thylacine photograph, unknown photographer (possibly Victor Prout), 1869; public domain.

Sunstar photograph by Cleveland Hickman; used with permission.

The Animal Globe pages are adapted from "Le Paper Globe," found at Joachim Robert's website: http://joachimesque.com/globe; used with permission. I have used them as templates to mark those missing species ravaged in modern times. Please cut out the globe pages and assemble according to the tab numbers. Clear tape seems to work best, though glue or a stapler will also do. The idea has always been that whatever poems or lists are on the other side will be destroyed or repurposed in the process.

Biosphere 2 photograph by CDO Ventures and the University of Arizona Biosphere 2; used with permission.

Passenger pigeon illustration (in parts) by John James Audubon; public domain.

"Eva at the Festival of Colors" photograph by Laird Hunt; used with permission.

GENERAL NOTES & QUOTES

"When a vision comes from the thunder beings of the west, it comes with terror like a thunderstorm; but when the storm of vision has passed, the world is greener and happier; for wherever the truth of vision comes upon the world, it is like a rain. The world, you see, is happier after the terror of the storm."

Biologists Humberto R. Maturana and Francisco J. Varela first introduced the term *autopoiesis* in a 1972 text called *De Máquinas y Seres Vivos* (in English, *Autopoiesis: The Organization of Living Systems*), later collected in *Autopoiesis and Cognition: The Realization of the Living* (Dordrecht/Boston: D. Reidel Publishing Company, 1980).

"Do Nothing Fancy" ends with a line by Bernadette Mayer, and something in "The book is the house" was inspired by Lisa Robertson. "It's a Saturday" ends with a line by Alice Notley.

Boxed questions in "Essay: Happy Brain" are the *d*'s on the Likert scale, adapted from *The Psychology of Happiness* by Michael Argyle, New York: Routledge, 1987.

The "Felicific Calculus" and happiness factors come from Jeremy Bentham ("If pains must come, let them extend to few").

The happy/sad corpus blog post is from "A Corpus-based Approach to Finding Happiness" by Rada Mihalcea and Hugo Liu. Kind permission granted by the authors.

That page (page 39), like the beginning of these notes, also contains a quote from *Black Elk Speaks* (as told through John G. Neihardt), New York: Washington Square Press, 1972. First published 1932.

I lifted the squirrel / twirl rhyme from Suzy Scarlata.

"La poésie est la mémoire de la langue" is from *Description du projet,* Jacques Roubaud, Caen: Editions Nous, 2014.

How to Assemble the Animal Globe begins and ends with a quote from John James Audubon's *Birds of America.*

Oracle or, utopia contains a quote from Robert Smithson quoting Sir Uvedale Price's *An Essay on the Picturesque,* from "Frederick Law Olmsted and the Dialectical Landscape," in *Robert Smithson: The Collected Writings,* Berkeley: University of California Press, 1996.

"All the length of the body and all its parts and functions were participating, and were being realized and rewarded, inseparable from the mind, identical with it: and all, everything, that the mind touched, was actuality, and all, everything, that the mind touched turned immediately, yet without in the least losing the quality of its total individuality, into joy and truth . . . revealed, of its self, truth, which in its very nature was joy, which must be the end of art, of investigation, and of all anyhow human existence."
   —James Agee (*Let Us Now Praise Famous Men,* New York: Mariner Books, 2001.
      First published 1941.)

Somewhere, I wanted to say: what will be remembered of some animals is a few bones, some pictures, YouTube videos, cryopreserved embryos, oocytes, induced pluripotent stem cells, some frozen tissues, their names, wiki entries,

and their poems.

The *Oracle or, utopia* section was inspired, in part, by a visit to Biosphere 2, an experiment in creating a living, materially autonomous world (autopoietic) capable of self-renewal under the right circumstances. Biosphere 1 is where we live now.

ACKNOWLEDGMENTS

I'd like to thank all those who read this book in manuscript at various stages and offered wise advice. In particular, and always, Laird Hunt. Also, Tim Atkins, Julie Carr, Rachel Feder, Chris Fischbach, Michael O, and Erika Stevens. Thanks to Carla Valadez and to Megan Mangum for their incredible attention to details.

A grant from the University of Denver, a Lannan residency at Marfa, time at Djerassi, and the sturdy generosity of Susie at Brown Bag Farms aided the writing and editing process over the years.

I'm grateful, too, to those editors devoted to the ongoing life of poetry, who took an interest in this work and published poems in their magazines, anthologies, and chapbooks or on audio sites. I hope I haven't forgotten any in this list.

Oracle or, utopia appeared as a chapbook from Horse Less Press, and *How to Assemble the Animal Globe* appeared as a chapbook from Nous-zōt.

Several poems appeared in the anthology *Futures: Poetry of the Greek Crisis* (London: Penned in the Margins, 2015) and its Greek version (Athens: Hestia Publishers, 2017). "Some of Us Got Lucky" appeared in *Hydrogen Jukebox: 40 Years of [Dis]embodied Poetics.* *Fact-Simile* made a poetry trading card of "who did the blue school." Portions of the rider appeared in an essay for *American Book Review.* Grace, thanks, and strength to those editors, and to the editors of *Banango Street, Boston Review, Brooklyn Rail, Cloud Rodeo, Conjunctions, Dream the End* (http://www.dreamtheend.com/?cat=656), *Dusie* Ecopoethos issue, *Grey, Helix Syntax* (Naropa Summer Writing Program), *one pause* (www.onepausepoetry.org), the Playground of the Americas Audio Arkhive (Fast Speaking Music), *Plume, The Plume Anthology of Poetry 3, READ* (Read Translation Seminars), Textsound, *Timber, Wave Composition,* and *West Branch.*

The cover image photo is by Laird Hunt, taken at the Festival of Colors (inspired by Hindu Holi), Φεστιβαλ Χρωματων Κεραπεικου–Μεταξουργειου, in the Kerameikos-Metaxourgeiou neighborhood of Athens, which once housed silk mills and is now a working-class, immigrant, and artists' neighborhood built on an ancient cemetery.

Coffee House Press began as a small letterpress operation in 1972 and has grown into an internationally renowned nonprofit publisher of literary fiction, essay, poetry, and other work that doesn't fit neatly into genre categories.

Coffee House is both a publisher and an arts organization. Through our *Books in Action* program and publications, we've become interdisciplinary collaborators and incubators for new work and audience experiences. Our vision for the future is one where a publisher is a catalyst and connector.

LITERATURE
is not the same thing as
PUBLISHING

FUNDER ACKNOWLEDGMENTS

Coffee House Press is an internationally renowned independent book publisher and arts nonprofit based in Minneapolis, MN; through its literary publications and *Books in Action* program, Coffee House acts as a catalyst and connector—between authors and readers, ideas and resources, creativity and community, inspiration and action.

Coffee House Press books are made possible through the generous support of grants and donations from corporations, state and federal grant programs, family foundations, and the many individuals who believe in the transformational power of literature. This activity is made possible by the voters of Minnesota through a Minnesota State Arts Board Operating Support grant, thanks to the legislative appropriation from the arts and cultural heritage fund, along with a grant from the Wells Fargo Foundation. Coffee House also receives major operating support from the Amazon Literary Partnership, the Bush Foundation, the Jerome Foundation, The McKnight Foundation, Target, and the National Endowment for the Arts (NEA). To find out more about how NEA grants impact individuals and communities, visit www.arts.gov.

Coffee House Press receives additional support from the Elmer L. & Eleanor J. Andersen Foundation; the David & Mary Anderson Family Foundation; the Buuck Family Foundation; the Carolyn Foundation; the Dorsey & Whitney Foundation; Dorsey & Whitney LLP; the Knight Foundation; the Rehael Fund of the Minneapolis Foundation; the Matching Grant Program Fund of the Minneapolis Foundation; the Schwab Charitable Fund; Schwegman, Lundberg & Woessner, P.A.; the Scott Family Foundation; the US Bank Foundation; VSA Minnesota for the Metropolitan Regional Arts Council; the Archie D. & Bertha H. Walker Foundation; and the Woessner Freeman Family Foundation in honor of Allan Kornblum.

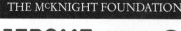

Make Yourself Happy was designed by
Megan Mangum, Words That Work.
Text is set in Whitney by Hoefler & Co. and
Dante MT, originally designed by Giovanni Mardersteig.